Keto Fat Cookbook

Low Carb Sweet and Savory Snacks to Boost Fat Burning
77 Keto Fat Bombs Recipes that Will Satisfy Your Hunger

Brandon Hearn © 2018

Table of Contents

Introduction

Before we get into what keto fat bombs are, you'll need to understand the keto diet. It's a low carb and high fat diet that allows for moderate protein. You have to reduce carbs before substituting it with fat. Your body currently runs on glucose which is an energy source that's easy for the body to use and it comes from carbs.

Your body will also run on insulin which is a hormone that processes the glucose in your bloodstream. With the ketogenic diet, you'll enter ketosis which is a natural process that your body uses to survive when your food intake it low. When your body is in ketosis, your body runs on ketones which it produces. You don't go into ketosis because of a lack of calories but it happens due to a lack of carbohydrates.

Types of Keto Diets

Below you'll find the four types of ketogenic diet, but this book will concentrate on the standard ketogenic diet.

- **Standard:** 75% Fat, 20% Protein, 5% Carbs
- **Cyclical:** This diet has five keto days by two high carb days.
- **High Protein:** 60% Fat, 35% Protein, 5% Carbs
- **Targeted:** This diet is where you'll add carbs just around physical workouts.

A Keto Reminder

In this section, we'll go over what foods you can and can't eat on the ketogenic diet. This is where fat bombs come in handy. Sometimes you won't have the time you need to cook a completely ketogenic meal, which is why fat bombs will help to get you through the day.

Can Eat:

- Alligator
- Bacon
- Bear
- Beef
- Bison
- Boar
- Chicken
- Crab
- Duck
- Eggs
- Elk
- Goa
- Goose
- Lamb
- Ham
- Kielbasa
- Lobster
- Mussels
- Oysters
- Pheasant salmon
- Quail
- Rabbit
- Scallop
- Shrimp
- Trout
- Turkey
- Turtle
- Most Fish
- Cheese
- Greek yogurt sour cream
- Heavy whipping cream
- Cream Cheese
- Artichoke
- Arugula
- Alfalfa Sprouts
- Bok Choy
- Beet Greens
- Banana Peppers
- Avocado
- Asparagus
- Broccoli
- Brussels Sprouts
- Lettuce
- Cabbage
- Cauliflower
- Celery
- Chard
- Chicory Greens
- Collard Greens
- Eggplant
- Cucumber
- Green beans
- Jalapeno
- Jicama
- Mushroom
- Mustard Greens
- Okra
- Radish

- Red Tomatoes
- Kale
- Most Squash
- Zucchini
- Tomatoes
- Strawberries
- Cranberries
- Mulberries
- Raspberries
- Blueberries
- Walnuts
- Sunflower
- Macadamias
- Seeds
- Monk Fruit Sweetener
- Xylitol
- Stevia
- Erythritol
- Animal Fats
- Avocado Oil
- Butter
- Cocoa Butter
- Flaxseed Oil
- Coconut Butter
- Ghee
- Hemp Oil
- Lard
- Macadamia Oil
- Mayonnaise
- Olive Oil
- Peanut Oil
- Pumpkin Seed Oil
- Sesame Oil
- Walnut Oil

Foods to Reduce or Avoid

- Wheat
- Corn
- Potatoes
- Rice
- Cereal
- Rye
- Oats
- Barley
- Millet
- Bulgur

-
- Amaranth
- Buckwheat
- Quinoa
- Honey
- Maple syrup
- Agave
- Apples
- Bananas
- Citrus (and Other Fruits)

What Fat Bombs Are

When you start the ketogenic diet, you'll encounter the word fat bomb. You probably are thinking that it's greasy bowls of junk food or ice cream, but this isn't the case. Keto fat bombs are a snack that are high in fat and low in both carbs and protein. They're the perfect snack for a low carb diet. It allows you to have an easy way to get the healthy fats that you need to stay on the ketogenic diet. To stay on the ketogenic diet, you have to have a certain percent of fat that can be difficult to get when you're busy. Fat bombs can be stored easily and made in advance, so you always have what you need to stay on the ketogenic diet.

They're Small

Fat bombs are small so that they're high in fat in a small portion. They're usually bite size but they can be up to the size of mini muffins depending on your recipe. You'll need molds to make fat bombs, but muffin liners will usually help as well.

They're Sweet or Savory

Fat bombs can be divided into these two groups. In these groups they'll include everything from breakfast to dessert flavors so that you can get something that fits the time of day and your current mood. You'll need low calorie sweeteners such as Swerve, stevia, and liquid stevia. Of course, you can use your own low carb.

Store them in the Fridge

Fat bombs are best kept in the fridge unless your recipes tells you to keep them in the freezer. Most fat bombs can be kept one to two weeks in your fridge so long as they're kept in an airtight container. Alternatively, most can be frozen and thawed as well, but this can make it more difficult to get them on the go.

They Can Have Nuts & Seeds

You're allowed nuts and seeds on the ketogenic diet, but you shouldn't get too many of them. They're rich in carbs, so you'll find that these are often higher in net carbs.

How to Use Them

Here are what you should use keto fat bombs

- **Energy:** Use them as a quick hit of energy, especially if you don't have time to cook. This can keep you from breaking your diet and eating out.
- **For Workouts:** You can use them as a pre or even post workout snack. It's better than regular snacks but they're not high in carbs.
- **Fat Intake:** You will want to use fat bombs to boost your fat intake when you're having a busy day.

Making Your Own Fat Bombs

There are three basic ingredients to every fat bomb.

- **Healthy Fat:** You'll need one of the following: cacao butter, coconut oil, coconut milk, coconut cream (the solid part that is on canned coconut milk once it's refrigerated), ghee, butter, bacon fat or avocado oil

- **Flavoring:** Vanilla Extract (Sugar Free), 100% Dark Chocolate, Cacao Powder, Sea Salt, Peppermint Extract, Spices or More

- **Texture:** Cacao Nibs, Pecans, Walnuts, Almonds, Chia Seeds, Bacon Bits, Shredded Coconut

Combine all ingredients in a bowl. You can also use a food processor or blender. If you're using a solid fat, you'll need to melt it in the microwave.

You will then shape it by either pouring it into a baking pan, muffin cup, mold or forming small balls as needed. Afterwards, refrigerate or freeze your fat bombs until they become solid. This can take several hours depending on your recipe.

Sweet Fat Bombs

Just because you're on a diet doesn't mean that you can't indulge your sweet tooth. Whenever you're craving something sweet, try one of these fat bombs on for size.

Easy Vanilla Bombs

Serves: 14 **Time:** 50 Minutes
Calories: 132 **Protein:** 0.8 Grams **Fat:** 14.4 Grams **Net Carbs:** 0.6 Grams
Ingredients:
- 1 Cup Macadamia Nuts, Unsalted
- ¼ Cup Coconut Oil / ¼ Cup Butter
- 2 Teaspoons Vanilla Extract, Sugar Free
- 20 Drops Liquid Stevia
- 2 Tablespoons Erythritol, Powdered

Directions:
1. Pulse your macadamia nuts in a blender, and then combine all of your ingredients together. Mix well.
2. Get out mini muffin tins with a tablespoon and a half of the mixture.
3. Refrigerate it for a half hour before serving.

Spiced Cocoa Bombs

Serves: 10 **Time:** 2 Hours 10 Minutes
Calories: 48.8 Grams
Protein: 0.7 Grams **Fat:** 5 Grams **Net Carbs:** 1.1 Grams
Ingredients:

- 1 Cup Coconut Milk
- 1 Teaspoon Vanilla Extract, Sugar Free
- 2 Tablespoons Cocoa Powder, Unsweetened
- ¼ Teaspoon Cayenne Pepper
- 1 Teaspoon Cinnamon
- 2 Tablespoon Erythritol
- 20 Drops Stevia Extract

Directions:

1. Warm your coconut milk, and then add all of your ingredients together.

2. Pour this into molds, and freeze for two hours before serving.

Pecan & Maple Bombs

Serves: 12 **Time:** 1 Hour 55 Minutes
Calories: 299 **Protein:** 4.74 Grams
Fat: 29.7 Grams **Net Carbs:** 2.51 Grams
Ingredients:
- ½ Cup Coconut Oil
- ¼ Cup Maple Syrup, Sugar Free
- 25 Drops Liquid Stevia
- ½ Cup Coconut, Shredded & Unsweetened
- ½ Cup Golden Flaxseed Meal
- 1 Cup Almond Flour
- 2 Cups Pecan Halves

Directions:
1. Start by heating your oven to 350, and then toast your pecans. They should take six to eight minutes. Allow them to cool before crushing them. Place them in a bowl and set it to the side.
2. Mix all of your dry ingredients with your pecans, and then add in your remaining ingredients. It should create a crumbly mixture.
3. Spread this in a prepared casserole dish, and then bake at 350 for twenty to twenty-five minutes.
4. Allow it to cool, and then refrigerate it for an hour before serving. Make sure to slice it first.

Spiced Peanut Butter Bombs

Serves: 2 **Time:** 2 Hours 5 Minutes
Calories: 186
Protein: 3.96 Grams **Fat:** 17.8 Grams **Net Carbs:** 3.26 Grams
Ingredients:

- 1 Teaspoon Cocoa Powder
- 1 Tablespoon Coconut Oil
- 1 tablespoon Heavy Cream
- 2 Tablespoons Peanut Butter
- ¼ Teaspoon Allspice
- 4-6 Drops Liquid Sucralose

Directions:

1. Combine all of your ingredients together, mixing well.
2. Freeze in molds for two hours.

Red Velvet Bombs

Serves: 25 **Time:** 55 Minutes
Calories: 85
Protein: 1 Gram **Fat:** 9 Grams **Net Carbs:** 1.2 Grams
Ingredients:

- 3.5 Ounces Dark Chocolate, 90%
- 1 Teaspoon Vanilla Extract, Sugar Free
- 4.5 Ounces Cream Cheese, Softened
- 3 Tablespoons Stevia
- 4 Drops Red Food Coloring
- 1/3 Cup Heavy Cream, Whipped

Directions:

1. Get out a heatproof bowl, melting your chocolate in ten second intervals in the microwave.

2. Combine all of your remaining ingredients except for the whipped cream. Use a hand mixer to make sure it's completely smooth.

3. Add your melted chocolate in, mixing for two minutes more.

4. Fill a piping bag with the mixture, transferring it into a lined tray, and then refrigerate it for forty minutes.

5. Top with whipped cream before serving.

Pistachio & Almond Bombs

Serves: 36 **Time:** 8 Hours 30 Minutes
Calories: 170
Protein: 2.2 Grams **Fat:** 17.4 Grams **Net Carbs:** 1.2 Grams
Ingredients:

- 1 Cup Almond Butter, Roasted
- ½ Cup Cacao Butter, Melted
- 1 Cup Creamy Coconut Butter
- ½ Cup Coconut Milk, Full Fat
- 1 Cup Coconut Oil, Firm
- ¼ Cup Ghee
- 1 Tablespoon Vanilla Extract, Pure
- 2 Teaspoons Chai Spice
- ¼ Cup Pistachios, Raw, Shelled & Chopped
- ¼ Teaspoon Himalayan Sea Salt
- ¼ Teaspoon Almond Extract, Pure

Directions:

1. Microwave your cacao butter until it melts, and then set it to the side.
2. Mix all ingredients except for your cacao butter and pistachios, making sure it's well combined.
3. Pour your cacao butter into the almond mixture, mixing well, and then transfer to a baking pan. Sprinkle it with pistachios, and refrigerate for eight hours or overnight.
4. Slice before serving.

Sweet Espresso Bombs

Serves: 24 **Time:** 4 Hours 20 Minutes
Calories: 63
Protein: 0.3 Grams **Fat:** 6.8 Grams **Net Carbs:** 0.3 Grams
Ingredients:
- 2 Tablespoons Heavy Whipping Cream
- 2 Tablespoons Stevia
- 4 Tablespoons Coconut Oil
- 3 Ounces Cream Cheese, Full Fat & Softened
- 2 Ounces Espresso
- 5 Tablespoons Butter, Unsalted & Softened

Directions:
1. Put your sweetener to the side and melt all of your ingredients in a double boiler. This should take three to four minutes. Make sure to mix well.

2. Add in your sweetener, mixing again

3. Spoon into muffin molds, freezing for four hours before serving.

Strawberry Shortcake Bombs

Serves: 6 **Time:** 1Hour 10 Minutes
Calories: 211
Protein: 1.5 Grams **Fat:** 13.5 Grams **Net Carbs:** 3.2 Grams
Ingredients:

- ¾ Cup Almond Flour
- ¼ Cup Coconut Flour
- ¼ Cup Coconut, Shredded
- ½ Cup Strawberries
- 1 Teaspoon Vanilla Extract, Pure
- 1 Tablespoon Coconut Oil
- 1 Teaspoon Stevia

Directions:

1. Blend all of your ingredients together except for your shredded coconut. Mix well.

2. Make into small bite sized balls, and roll them in your shredded coconut.

3. Freeze for at least an hour before serving.

Blueberry Cream Bombs

Serves: 15 **Time:** 2 Hours 10 Minutes
Calories: 241
Protein: 0.8 Grams **Fat:** 12.2 Grams **Net Carbs:** 6.1 Grams
Ingredients:

- 4 Ounces Goat Cheese
- ½ Cup Blueberries, Fresh
- ½ Teaspoon Stevia
- ¼ Cup Coconut, Shredded & Unsweetened
- ½ Cup Pecans
- 1 Teaspoon Vanilla Extract, Pure
- 1 Cup Almond Flour

Directions:

1. Throw all of your ingredients into a blender, and blend well.

2. Make thirty balls out of this mixture, and roll it into coconut flakes.

3. Freeze for at least an hour before serving.

Blackberry Coconut Bombs

Serves: 6 **Time:** 1 Hour 15 Minutes
Calories: 225 **Protein:** 5.2 Grams
Fat: 12.7 Grams **Net Carbs:** 4.7 Grams
Ingredients:

- 1 Cup Coconut Butter
- 1 Cup Coconut Oil
- ½ Cup Blackberries, Frozen
- 1 Tablespoon Lemon Juice
- ¼ Teaspoon Vanilla Powder
- ½ Teaspoon Stevia Drops

Directions:

1. Add your coconut oil, coconut butter and blackberries into a cooking pot, cooking until it's mixed well.

2. Transfer this mixture into a blender, adding in all of your remaining ingredients.

3. Blend until smooth, and then get out a six inch pan.

4. Line a pan with parchment paper, and then pour your blackberry mixture into the pan. Spread it out evenly, and refrigerate for at least an hour.

5. Remove from the pan, slicing into squares before serving.

Peaches & Cream Bombs

Serves: 6 **Time:** 2 Hours 10 Minutes
Calories: 209 **Protein:** 6.2 Grams
Fat: 13.2 Grams **Net Carbs:** 0.6 Grams
Ingredients:

- 1 Ounce Cream Cheese, Softened
- 2 Tablespoons Butter, Softened
- ¼ Cup Swerve
- 2 Tablespoons Heavy Whipping Cream
- 4 Ounces Mascarpone, Softened
- ½ Teaspoon Peach Extract
- 2 Ounces Peaches, Diced Fine

Directions:

1. Blend your butter, cream cheese and mascarpone in a blender until mixed well.

2. Stir in your vanilla, sweetener and peach extract. Mix well, and then divide between your silicone molds.

3. Freeze for at least two hours before serving.

Sweet Ginger Bombs

Serves: 12 **Time:** 2 Hours 5 Minutes
Calories: 79 **Protein:** 0 Grams
Fat: 9 Grams **Net Carbs:** 1 Gram
Ingredients:

- 4 Ounces Coconut, Shredded
- 2 Ounces Coconut Oil
- 2 Ounces Butter, Grass Fed
- 1 Tablespoon Ginger, Grated
- 1 Teaspoon Cinnamon
- 1 Teaspoon Vanilla Extract, Pure
- ½ Tablespoon Roasted Cashews, Crushed
- Stevia to Taste
- Pinch Sea Salt

Directions:

1. Start by softening your coconut oil and butter.

2. Mix all ingredients together until smooth and blended well.

3. Pour into molds and freeze before serving.

Custard Cups

Serves: 12 **Time:** 45 Minutes
Calories: 349 **Protein:** 2 Grams **Fat:** 37 Grams **Net Carbs:** 4 Grams
Ingredients:

- 2 Tablespoons Gelatin
- 1 ½ Teaspoons Vanilla Extract, Pure
- 6 Eggs Xylitol
- 5 Egg Yolks
- Stevia to Taste
- ¼ Cup Protein Powder, Vanilla
- ½ Cup Coconut Oil
- ½ Cup Coconut, Shredded
- 2 Cups Coconut Milk
- ½ lb. Butter, Grass Fed

Directions:

1. Start by beating your egg yolks until they are creamy and smooth.
2. Melt your coconut toil and butter together, and then add in your coconut milk. Mix well.
3. Add in your gelatin, and stir until it thickens and dissolves.
4. Remove it from heat, allowing it to cool. Stir in your protein powder and vanilla extract.
5. Add in your egg yolks, and then remove it from heat.
6. Stir in your vanilla extract and protein powder.
7. Pour into bowls, sprinkling your coconut on top.
8. Chill until you're ready to serve.

Nutty White Chocolate Bites

Serves: 12 **Time:** 2 Hours 5 Minutes
Calories: 92 **Protein:** 0 Grams **Fat:** 10 Grams **Net Carbs:** 1 Gram
Ingredients:

- 4 Tablespoons Cocoa Butter
- 4 Tablespoons Coconut Butter
- ½ Cup Roasted Pecans, Chopped
- 4 Tablespoons Coconut Oil
- 1 Teaspoon Scraped Vanilla Bean
- Liquid Stevia to taste
- Stevia to Taste
- Pinch Sea Salt

Directions:

1. Combine all of your ingredients together, pouring it into a bread pan that you've lined with parchment paper.

2. Freeze for one to two hours so that it sets.

3. Cut into squares and sprinkle with stevia before serving.

Fluffy Bites

Serves: 12
Time: 1 Hour 20 Minutes
Calories: 363
Protein: 2 Grams
Fat: 40 Grams
Net Carbs: 1 Gram
Ingredients:

- 2 Teaspoons Cinnamon
- 2/3 Cup Sour Cream
- 2 Cups Heavy Cream
- 1 Teaspoon Scraped Vanilla Bean
- ¼ Teaspoon Cardamom
- 4 Egg Yolks
- Stevia to Taste

Directions:

1. Start by whisking your egg yolks until creamy and smooth.

2. Get out a double boiler, and add your eggs with the rest of your ingredients. Mix well.

3. Remove from heat, allowing it to cool until it reaches room temperature.

4. Refrigerate for an hour before whisking well.

5. Pour into molds, and freeze for at least an hour before serving.

Mint Bites

Serves: 12 **Time:** 2 Hours 45 Minutes
Calories: 251 **Protein:** 3 Grams
Fat: 25 Grams **Net Carbs:** 6 Grams
Ingredients:

- 1 ½ Cups Coconut Oil
- 1 Cup Dark Chocolate Chips, Sugar Free
- 1 ¼ Cup Almond Butter
- 2 Teaspoons Vanilla Extract, Pure
- ½ Cup Parsley
- 1 Teaspoon Peppermint Extract
- Pinch Sea Salt
- Stevia to Taste

Directions:

1. Melt your coconut oil and dark chocolate chips together using a double boiler.

2. Add all ingredients into a blender, pulsing until smooth.

3. Pour into molds before freezing.

Cinnamon Apple Rounds

Serves: 12 **Time:** 3 Hours 10 Minutes
Calories: 168 **Protein:** 0 Grams
Fat: 12 Grams **Net Carbs:** 8 Grams
Ingredients:
- 1 Teaspoon Cinnamon
- 2 Tablespoons Coconut Oil
- 5 Ounces Heavy Cream
- ½ Cup Butter, Grass Fed
- 2 Apples
- Pinch of Sea Salt
- Stevia to Taste

Directions:
1. Slice your apples thin, and then get out a pan.
2. Melt your coconut oil, and then add in your apples and cinnamon. Mix until your apple slices are well coated.
3. Cook the mixture until your apple slices become tender, and then mash them gently with your spoon.
4. Remove the mixture from heat and fold in the remaining ingredients.
5. Pour it into candy molds, and then freeze for three hours.
6. Store in the fridge until you're ready to serve.

Creamy Clouds

Serves: 5 **Time:** 1 Hour 5 Minutes
Calories: 134 **Protein:** 1 Gram
Fat: 14 Grams **Net Carbs:** 0 Grams
Ingredients:

- ½ Cup Butter, Grass Fed
- 8 Ounces Cream Cheese
- ½ Teaspoon Vanilla Extract, Pure
- Stevia to Taste

Directions:

1. Whisk all of your ingredients together until they form a frothy mixture. You'll want to use an electric beater.

2. Drop it into spoonsfuls on a tray, and freeze until it sets.

Spicy Pumpkin Bombs

Serves: 12 **Time:** 8 Hours 20 Minutes
Calories: 99 **Protein:** 2 Grams
Fat: 10 Grams **Net Carbs:** 1 Gram
Ingredients:

- ½ Cup Pumpkin, Diced
- 3 Tablespoons Coconut Butter
- 1 ½ Tablespoons Coconut Oil
- ¼ Teaspoon Ginger
- ¼ Teaspoon Nutmeg
- ¼ Teaspoon Cinnamon
- 1/8 Teaspoon Cloves
- Stevia to Taste

Directions:

1. Melt your coconut butter and oil together, and whisk well.
2. Add in your stevia, whisking again until it turns smooth.
3. Add in your diced pumpkin and the spices to a blender, blending until it's chopped into small pieces.
4. Mix together, stirring well.
5. Make small balls, and then place them on parchment paper.
6. Allow them to set in the fridge before serving.

Coconut Fudge

Serves: 12 **Time:** 2 Hours 20 Minutes
Calories: 172 **Protein:** 0 Grams
Fat: 20 Grams **Net Carbs:** 0 Grams
Ingredients:

- 2 Cups Coconut Oil
- ½ Cup Dark Cocoa Powder
- ½ Cup Coconut Cream
- ¼ Cup Almonds, Chopped
- ¼ Cup Coconut, Shredded
- 1 Teaspoon Almond Extract
- Pinch of Salt
- Stevia to Taste

Directions:

1. Pour your coconut oil and coconut cream in a bowl, whisking with an electric beater until smooth. Once the mixture becomes smooth and glossy, do not continue.

2. Begin to add in your cocoa powder while mixing slowly, making sure that there aren't any lumps.

3. Add in the rest of your ingredients, and mix well.

4. Line a bread pan with parchment paper, and freeze until it sets.

5. Slice into squares before serving.

Nutmeg Nougat

Serves: 12 **Time:** 2 Hours 50 Minutes
Calories: 341 **Protein:** 3 Grams
Fat: 34 Grams **Net Carbs:** 5 Grams
Ingredients:
- 1 Cup Heavy Cream
- 1 Cup Cashew Butter
- 1 Cup Coconut, Shredded
- ½ Teaspoon Nutmeg
- 1 Teaspoon Vanilla Extract, Pure
- Stevia to Taste

Directions:
1. Melt your cashew butter using a double boiler, and then stir in your vanilla extract, dairy cream, nutmeg and stevia. Make sure it's mixed well.

2. Remove from heat, allowing it to cooldown before refrigerating it for a half hour.

3. Shape into balls, and coat with shredded coconut. Chill for at least two hours before serving.

Sweet Almond Bites

Serves: 12 **Time:** 2 Hours 10 Minutes
Calories: 350 **Protein:** 2 Grams
Fat: 38 Grams **Net Carbs:** 0 Grams
Ingredients:

- 18 Ounces Butter, Grass Fed
- 2 Ounces Heavy Cream
- ½ Cup Stevia
- 2/3 Cup Cocoa Powder
- 1 Teaspoon Vanilla Extract, Pure
- 4 Tablespoons Almond Butter

Directions:

1. Use a double boiler to melt your butter before adding in all of your remaining ingredients.

2. Place the mixture into molds, freezing for two hours before serving.

Strawberry Cheesecake Minis

Serves: 12 **Time:** 3 Hours 10 Minutes
Calories: 372 **Protein:** 1 Gram
Fat: 41 Grams **Net Carbs:** 2 Grams
Ingredients:
- 1 Cup Coconut Oil
- 1 Cup Coconut Butter
- ½ Cup Strawberries, Sliced
- ½ Teaspoon Lime Juice
- 2 Tablespoons Cream Cheese, Full Fat
- Stevia to Taste

Directions:
1. Blend your strawberries together.

2. Soften your cream cheese, and then add in your coconut butter.

3. Combine all ingredients together, and then pour your mixture into silicone molds.

4. Freeze for at least two hours before serving.

Cocoa Brownies

Serves: 12 **Time:** 40 Minutes
Calories: 184 **Protein:** 1 Gram
Fat: 20 Grams **Net Carbs:** 1 Gram
Ingredients:

- 1 Egg
- 2 Tablespoons Butter, Grass Fed
- 2 Teaspoons Vanilla Extract, Pure
- ¼ Teaspoon Baking Powder
- ¼ Cup Cocoa Powder
- 1/3 Cup Heavy Cream
- ¾ Cup Almond Butter
- Pinch Sea Salt

Directions:

1. Break your egg into a bowl, whisking until smooth.

2. Add in all of your wet ingredients, mixing well.

3. Mix all dry ingredients into a bowl.

4. Sift your dry ingredients into your wet ingredients, mixing to form a batter.

5. Get out a baking pan, greasing it before pouring in your mixture.

6. Heat your oven to 350 and bake for twenty-five minutes.

7. Allow it to cool before slicing and serve room temperature or warm.

Chocolate Orange Bites

Serves: 12 **Time:** 2 Hours 10 Minutes
Calories: 188 **Protein:** 1 Gram
Fat: 21 Grams **Net Carbs:** 1 Gram
Ingredients:
- 10 Ounces Coconut Oil
- 4 Tablespoons Cocoa Powder
- ¼ Teaspoon Blood Orange Extract
- Stevia to Taste

Directions:
1. Melt half of your coconut oil using a double boiler, and then add in your stevia and orange extract.

2. Get out candy molds, pouring the mixture into it. Fill each mold halfway, and then place in the fridge until they set.

3. Melt the other half of your coconut oil, stirring in your cocoa powder and stevia, making sure that the mixture is smooth with no lumps.

4. Pour into your molds, filling them up all the way, and then allow it to set in the fridge before serving.

Caramel Cones

Serves: 12 **Time:** 2 Hours 5 Minutes
Calories: 100 **Protein:** 0 Grams
Fat: 12 Grams **Net Carbs:** 1 Gram
Ingredients:

- 2 Tablespoons Heavy Whipping Cream
- 2 Tablespoons Sour Cream
- 1 Tablespoon Caramel Sugar
- 1 Teaspoon Sea Salt, Fine
- 1/3 Cup Butter, Grass Fed
- 1/3 Cup Coconut Oil
- Stevia to Taste

Directions:
1. Soften your coconut oil and butter, mixing together.

2. Mix all ingredients together to form a batter, and ten place them in mol.ds.

3. Top with a little salt, and keep refrigerated until serving.

Cinnamon Bites

Serves: 12 **Time:** 2 Hours 5 Minutes
Calories: 165 **Protein:** 1 Gram
Fat: 18 Grams **Net Carbs:** 1 Gram
Ingredients:

- 1/8 Teaspoon Nutmeg
- 1 Teaspoon Vanilla Extract
- ¼ Teaspoon Cinnamon
- 4 Tablespoons Coconut Oil
- ½ Cup Butter, Grass Fed
- 8 Ounces Cream Cheese
- Stevia to Taste

Directions:

1. Soften your coconut oil and butter, mixing in your cream cheese.

2. Add all of your remaining ingredients, and mix well.

3. Pour into molds, and freeze until set.

Sweet Chai Bites

Serves: 12 **Time:** 2 Hours 5 Minutes
Calories: 178 **Protein:** 1 Gram
Fat: 19 Grams **Net Carbs:** 1 Gram
Ingredients:

- 1 Cup Cream Cheese
- 1 Cup Coconut Oil
- 2 Ounces Butter, Grass Fed
- 2 Teaspoons Ginger
- 2 Teaspoons Cardamom
- 1 Teaspoon Nutmeg
- 1 Teaspoon Cloves
- 1 Teaspoon Vanilla Extract, Pure
- 1 Teaspoon Darjeeling Black Tea
- Stevia to Taste

Directions:

1. Melt your coconut oil and butter before adding in your black tea. Allow it to set for one to two minutes.

2. Add in your cream cheese, removing your mixture from heat.

3. Add in all of your spices, and stir to combine.

4. Pour into molds, and freeze before serving.

Ice Cream Bombs

Serves: 12 **Time:** 2 Hours 10 Minutes
Calories: 250 **Protein:** 11 Grams
Fat: 19 Grams **Net Carbs:** 8 Grams
Ingredients:
- 1 Cup Cashew Butter
- 1 Cup Whipped Cream
- 3 Cups Protein Powder, Any Flavor
- Stevia to Taste

Directions:
1. Gently fold your protein powder into your whipped crema.

2. Add in your cashew butter and stevia.

3. Mix well, pouring into silicone molds. Freeze before serving.

Chocolate & Coconut Fudge

Serves: 12 **Time:** 8 Hours 10 Minutes
Calories: 78 **Protein:** 1 Gram
Fat: 8 Grams **Net Carbs:** 3 Grams
Ingredients:
- 1/3 Cup Dark Chocolate Chips
- ½ Cup Cocoa Powder
- ¼ Cup Coconut Milk, Full Fat
- ½ Cup Coconut Oil
- 1 Teaspoon Vanilla Extract, Pure
- Stevia to Taste

Directions:
1. Melt your coconut oil, placing it in a blender.
2. Add in the rest of your ingredients, blending until smooth and creamy.
3. Line a bread pan using parchment paper, pouring your mixture in.
4. Allow it to refrigerate for eight hours or overnight before slicing into twelve squares. Store in the fridge before serving.

Pecan & Maple Bars

Serves: 12 **Time:** 35 Minutes
Calories: 302 **Protein:** 5 Grams
Fat: 30 Grams **Net Carbs:** 2 Grams
Ingredients:

- 2 Cups Pecans, Chopped
- ½ Cup Chocolate Chips, Sugar Free
- 1 Cup Almond Meal
- ½ Cup Flaxseed Meal
- ½ Cup Coconut Oil, Warmed
- ½ Cup Maple Syrup, Sugar Free
- 20-25 Drops Liquid Stevia

Directions:

1. Heat your oven to 350, and then bake your pecans until aromatic. This can take from six to eight minutes.

2. Sift all dry ingredients together, and then add in your roasted pecans. Mix well.

3. Line a bread pan with parchment paper.

4. Mix your maple syrup and coconut oil into the dry mixture until it becomes sticky and thick.

5. Pour into your prepared bread pan, baking for eighteen minutes.

6.   The top should brown, and slice to enjoy.

Pumpkin Pie Bombs

Serves: 12 **Time:** 3 Hours 40 Minutes
Calories: 124 **Protein:** 3 Grams
Fat: 13 Grams **Net Carbs:** 2 Grams
Ingredients:
- 3 Ounces Dark Chocolate, Sugar Free
- 1 ¼ Cup Almond Oil
- 1/3 Cup Almond Butter
- 1/3 Cup Pumpkin Puree
- 1 ½ Teaspoon Pumpkin Pie Spice
- 2 Tablespoons Coconut Oil
- Stevia to Taste

Directions:
1. Melt your almond oil and dark chocolate together using a double boiler.

2. Get out twelve muffin cups, and layer this mixture on the bottom. Freeze until your crust has set.

3. During this time get out a saucepan, placing it over low heat.

4. Combine all of your remaining ingredients, heating it until softened and mixed well.

5. Pour this into your chocolate mixture, and allow it to freeze for at least an hour before serving.

Chocolate Peanut Butter Bites

Serves: 12 **Time:** 32 Minutes
Calories: 148 **Protein:** 4 Grams
Fat: 13 Grams **Net Carbs:** 2 Grams
Ingredients:

- 2 Cups Almond Flour/ 1/3 Cup Crunch Peanut Butter
- 4 Ounces Dark Chocolate, Sugar Free
- ¼ Cup Coconut Oil, Warmed
- 3 Tablespoons Maple Syrup, Sugar Free
- 1 Tablespoon Vanilla Extract, Pure
- 1 ¼ Teaspoon Baking Powder
- Pinch Sea Salt/ Stevia to Taste

Directions:
1. Get out a large bowl, whisking together all wet ingredients. Mix until they turn light brown.
2. Get out a different bowl, mixing all of your dry ingredients except for your chocolate.
3. Sift your dry ingredients into the wet ingredients, mixing well. This should form a smooth batter before becoming crumbly.
4. Form this mixture into balls, wrapping each one with plastic wrap, and refrigerate for an hour.
5. Cut your chocolate into one inch pieces, and put a piece in the middle of each ball.
6. Line a baking tray, and heat your oven to 350.
7. Bake for eighteen minutes, and sprinkle with cinnamon before serving.

Chocolate Bacon

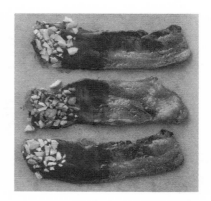

Serves: 12 **Time:** 1 Hour
Calories: 157 **Protein:** 10 Grams
Fat: 11 Grams **Net Carbs:** 1 Gram **Ingredients:**
Bacon:

- 1 Tablespoon Maple Syrup, Sugar Free
- 12 Bacon Slices
- Stevia to Taste

Coating:

- 15-20 Drops Liquid Stevia
- 4 Tablespoons Dark Cocoa Powder
- ¼ Cup Pecans, Chopped

Directions:

1. Lay your bacon on a baking tray in a single layer, rubbing your stevia and maple over each side of the slices.
2. Heat your oven to 275, and bake for ten to fifteen minutes. They should become crispy.
3. Drain your bacon grease away and reserve it.
4. Mix your bacon grease with your stevia and cocoa powder to form a coating.
5. Dip your bacon n this mixture, rolling it into your pecans.
6. Allow it to dry until it hardens.

Chocolate & Matcha Cups

Serves: 12 **Time:** 2 Hours 10 Minutes
Calories: 135 **Protein:** 1 Gram
Fat: 14 Grams **Net Carbs:** 1 Gram
Ingredients:
- 10 Ounces Dark Chocolate Chips
- ¼ Cup Butter, Grass Fed
- ½ Teaspoon Matcha (Green Tea Powder)
- 2 Teaspoons Coconut Oil
- Stevia to Taste

Directions:
1. Melt your chocolate chips using a double boiler, adding in your coconut oil. Stir well.

2. Grease a muffin tray, and brush the chocolate mixture onto the sides, freezing it for an hour.

3. During that time soften your butter, mixing in your stevia and matcha powder.

4. When the cups are set, then add in your matcha mixture, and refrigerate before serving.

Nut Nougats Bites

Serves: 12

Time: 1 Hour 10 Minutes

Calories: 367

Protein: 3 Grams

Fat: 28 Grams

Net Carbs: 3 Grams

Ingredients:

- 2 Ounces Walnuts, Chopped
- 4 Ounces Cocoa Butter
- 2 Ounces Macadamia Nuts, Chopped
- 2 Ounces Pecans, Chopped
- 1 Cup Heavy Cream
- 2 Tablespoons Cocoa Powder
- Stevia to Taste

Directions:

1. Melt your cocoa butter over a double boiler, mixing in your stevia and cocoa powder. It should form a smooth mixture, and make sure it's well combined. Remove from heat.

2. Whisk in your cream before folding in all of your nuts.

3. Pour this mixture into molds, allowing it to set in the fridge before serving.

Blueberry Bites

Serves: 12 **Time:** 4 Hours 15 Minutes
Calories: 77 **Protein:** 1 Gram **Fat:** 8 Grams **Net Carbs:** 1 Gram
Ingredients:
Filling:

- ¼ Teaspoon Cinnamon
- 1 Tablespoon Cacao Powder
- 1 Tablespoon Coconut Oil
- 2 Tablespoons Almond Butter
- Stevia to Taste
- Pinch Sea Salt, Fine

Topping:

- ¼ Cup Blueberries, Pureed
- ¼ Cup Cream Cheese
- ¼ Cup Butter, Grass Fed
- 1 Tablespoon Heavy Whipping Cream
- 1 Teaspoon Vanilla Extract, Pure

Directions:

1. Combine all of your filling ingredients together, mixing well.
2. Line a bread pan with parchment paper, spreading your filling mixture evenly in it. Freeze until it sets.
3. Add all topping ingredients to a blender, blending well.

4.   Remove your base from the freezer cutting it into squares before spreading the topping over each piece. Keep in the freezer until you're ready to serve.

Sweet Lemon Bombs

Serves: 12 **Time:** 2 Hours 5 Minutes
Calories: 75 **Protein:** 2 Grams **Fat:** 8 Grams **Net Carbs:** 1 Gram
Ingredients:
- ¼ Cup Butter, Grass Fed
- 4 Lemons
- Stevia to Taste
- ¼ Cup Coconut Oil
- 4 Ounces Cream Cheese, Full Fat
- Stevia to Taste

Directions:
1. Grate your lemon for zest and juice them.

2. Throw all of your ingredients into a blender, blending until well combined.

3. Pour into molds, and freeze until set.

Sweet Lime Pie

Serves: 12 **Time:** 2 Hours 15 Minutes
Calories: 146 **Protein:** 3 Grams **Fat:** 15 Grams **Net Carbs:** 1 Gram
Ingredients:
Crust:
- 1 Tablespoon Cinnamon
- ½ Teaspoon Vanilla Extract, Pure
- 3 Tablespoons Butter
- 1 Cup Almond Flour
- Stevia to Taste

Filling:
- 4 Ounces Cream Cheese, Full Fat
- 3 Tablespoons Butter
- 2 Limes
- ¼ Cup Coconut Oil
- Stevia to Taste

Directions:
1. Mix all of your crust ingredients together until the consistency is crumbly.
2. Press this mixture into twelve muffin cups, and then heat your oven to 350 degrees. Bake for seven minutes.
3. Juice and grate your lime for the zest. Add it to a food processor with your filling ingredients. Blend until smooth.
4. Once your crusts are cooked and cools, pour the mixture in the center.
5. Freeze until set, and keep in the fridge until you're ready to serve.

Peppermint Fudge

Serves: 12 **Time:** 8 Hours 10 Minutes
Calories: 206 **Protein:** 0 Grams **Fat:** 24 Grams
Net Carbs: 0 Grams
Ingredients:

- 10 Ounces Coconut Oil
- ½ Teaspoon Peppermint Extract
- 4 Tablespoons Cocoa powder
- 2 Tablespoons Stevia

Directions:

1. Combine all ingredients together, making sure it's mixed well.

2. Place them in ice trays, and refrigerate overnight before serving.

Sweet Fennel Bites

Serves: 12 **Time:** 3 Hours 5 Minutes
Calories: 172 **Protein:** 1 Gram
Fat: 20 Grams **Net Carbs:** 0 Grams
Ingredients:

- ¼ Cup Almond Milk
- 1 Teaspoon Vanilla Extract, Pure
- 1 Teaspoon Fennel Seeds
- ¼ Cup Cacao Powder
- ¼ Cup Coconut Oil
- Pinch Sea Salt, Fine

Directions:

1. Mix your coconut oil until it's smooth and glossy, and then mix in the rest of your ingredients.

2. Pour this into a piping bag, and line a baking tray with parchment paper.

3. Pipe into twelve dollops, and freeze for three hours.

4. Refrigerate until you're ready to serve.

White Chocolate Bites

Serves: 12 **Time:** 1 Hour 20 Minutes

Calories: 287 **Protein:** 1 Gram

Fat: 30 Grams **Net Carbs:** 1 Gram **Ingredients:**

Filling:

- 4 Ounces Cocoa Butter
- 6 Tablespoons Butter
- 1 ½ Cups Pecans, Chopped
- 6 Tablespoons Coconut Oil
- ¾ Teaspoon Vanilla Extract
- 1/8 Teaspoon Sea Salt, Fine
- Stevia to Taste

Coating:

- 1/8 Teaspoon Vanilla Extract, Pure
- 1/8 Teaspoon Stevia Extract
- 1 Ounce White Baking Chocolate, Unsweetened

- ¼ Ounce Cocoa Butter

Directions:
1. Melt your cocoa powder, coconut oil and butter using a double boiler, mixing well.
2. Add all remaining ingredients for your filling, and mix well.
3. Pour it into molds, and refrigerate overnight.
4. Next you'll prepare your white chocolate coating by melting your butter and chocolate together in a double boiler. Once melted, add in your stevia and vanilla.
5. Remove the base from your molds, dipping it into your coating.
6. Allow it to set in the fridge for at least two to three hours before serving.

Sweet Macaroons

Serves: 12 **Time:** 25 Minutes
Calories: 46
Protein: 2 Grams **Fat:** 5 Grams **Net Carbs:** Less Than 1 Gram
Ingredients:

- ½ Cup Coconut Flakes
- ¼ Cup Almond Meal
- 3 Egg Whites
- 1 Teaspoon Vanilla Extract, Pure
- 1 Tablespoon Coconut Oil
- 3 Egg Whites
- Stevia to Taste

Directions:

1. Mix all dry ingredients together, sifting them.
2. Melt your coconut oil, mixing in your vanilla extract.
3. Pour this into your dry mixture, and then beat your egg whites until they form stiff peaks.
4. Fold your egg whites into your mixture.
5. Line a baking sheet with parchment paper, making twelve dollops from your mixture.
6. Heat your oven to 400, and then bake for eight minutes.

Coconut Lime Bombs

Serves: 12 **Time:** 3 Hours 5 Minutes
Calories: 122 **Protein:** 1 Gram
Fat: 14 Grams **Net Carbs:** 1 Grams
Ingredients:

- 2 Ounces Cream Cheese, Full Fat
- ½ Ounce Coconut Flakes
- ½ Cup Coconut Oil
- ¼ Cup Butter, Grass Fed
- 2 Tablespoons Coconut Cream
- 2 Teaspoon Vanilla Extract, Pure
- 2 Limes
- Stevia to Taste

Directions:

1. Juice and grate our lime for the zest.
2. Melt your coconut oil and butter together, and then remove it from heat. Add in your cream cheese, mixing well.
3. Add all remaining ingredients except for your coconut flakes, mixing well.
4. Put your coconut flakes in a plate, rolling the mixture in them to coat them.
5. Freeze before serving.

Mocha Mascarpone Bombs

Serves: 12 **Time:** 3 Hours 10 Minutes
Calories: 77 **Protein:** 1 Gram
Fat: 8 Grams **Net Carbs:** 1 Gram
Ingredients:
- ½ Cup Mascarpone Cheese
- 3 Tablespoon Stevia
- 2 Tablespoons Butter, Grass Fed
- 1 Tablespoon Coconut Oil
- 1 ½ Tablespoons Cocoa Powder, Divided
- ½ Teaspoon Rum
- ¼ Teaspoon Instant Coffee
- Stevia to Taste

Directions:
1. Reserve a half a tablespoon of cocoa powder, and then place all of your ingredients into a blender. Pulse until creamy and smooth.
2. Pour this mixture into silicone molds, sprinkling with your reserved powder.
3. Freeze until you're ready to serve.

Strawberry & Cherry Bombs

Serves: 12 **Time:** 2 Hours 5 Minutes
Calories: 78 **Protein:** 0 Grams
Fat: 9 Grams **Net Carbs:** 0 Grams
Ingredients:

- 2 Ounces Half & Half
- 4 Tablespoons Coconut Oil
- 4 Cherries, Pitted
- 4 Strawberries, Diced
- 4 Tablespoons Grass Fed Butter
- Stevia to Taste

Directions:

1. Add your strawberries and cherries into a blender, blending until pureed.
2. Add in your stevia and half and half. Blend until it's mixed well.
3. Melt your butter using a double boiler, and then add it to the mixture.
4. Add in your coconut oil, mixing well.
5. Place your mixture into a piping bag, making twelve droplets on a prepared baking tray.
6. Freeze for two hours before serving. Keep frozen.

Coconut & Chocolate Bombs

Serves: 12 **Time:** 1 Hour 20 Minutes
Calories: 126 **Protein:** 0 Grams
Fat: 14 Grams **Net Carbs:** 0 Grams
Ingredients:

- ½ Cup Dark Chocolate Cocoa Powder
- 1 Cup Coconut Oil, Solid
- ½ Teaspoon Vanilla Extract, Pure
- 1 Teaspoon Peppermint Extract
- 5 Drops Stevia
- Pinch Sea Salt, Fine

Directions:

1. Blend all of your ingredients together in a blender, and then make twelve drops on a parchment paper lined baking sheet.

2. Refrigerate for at least an hour before serving.

Sweet Peanut Butter Bombs

Serves: 12 **Time:** 40 Minutes
Calories: 93 **Protein:** 2 Grams
Fat: 9 Grams **Net Carbs:** 2 Grams
Ingredients:
- ½ Cup Coconut, Shredded & Unsweetened
- 2 Tablespoons Butter, Grass Fed
- ¼ Cup Creamy Peanut Butter, Unsweetened
- 2-3 Drops Stevia
- ½ Cup Peanuts, Crushed
- ¼ Teaspoon Sea Salt, Fine
- 1 Cup Coconut Flour, Sifted

Directions:
1. Get out a stockpot and add in your peanut butter, butter, coconut oil and stevia heat it up over medium heat, and whisk until it's well blended.
2. Add in your coconut flour, salt and coconut. Stir well.
3. Transfer this mix to a bowl, and chill in the fridge for a half hour.
4. Add your crushed peanuts to a bowl while it's chilling.
5. Roll the balls into your crushed peanuts.

Chocolate Cream Cheese

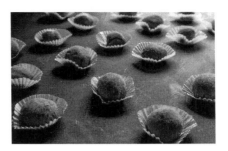

Serves: 12 **Time:** 3 Hours 5 Minutes
Calories: 100 **Protein:** 2 Grams
Fat: 10 Grams **Net Carbs:** 2 Grams
Ingredients:
- ½ Cup Dark Chocolate, Grated
- ½ Cup Walnuts, Chopped
- ½ Cup Cream Cheese, Full Fat
- Stevia To Taste

Filling:
- 4 Tablespoons Butter, Grass Fed
- 2 Tablespoons Espresso Powder
- 2 Tablespoons Heavy Cream
- Stevia to Taste

Directions:
1. Mix your dark chocolate and cream cheese together. You'll want to soften your cream cheese first, and then add in your chopped nuts and stevia. Mix well.
2. Get out twelve mini cupcake liners, and line the sides with the mixture. Make sure you make a crater, and then freeze for two hours.
3. Whip all filling ingredients together, and then fill each cream cheese crater with the filling before serving.

Savory Fat Bombs

You've had the sweet, so now try out some savory fat bombs that are great for when you aren't dealing with a sweet tooth.

Sausage Balls

Serves: 20 **Time:** 20 Minutes
Calories: 124 **Protein:** 6 Grams
Fat: 11 Grams **Net Carbs:** 0.2 Grams
Ingredients:
- 1 lb. Breakfast Sausage
- 1 Cup Almond Flour
- 1 Egg
- ¼ Cup Parmesan, Grated
- 1 Tablespoon Butter
- 2 Teaspoons Baking Powder

Directions:
1. Start by heating your oven to 350, and then get out a bowl.
2. Mix all of your ingredients together before making twenty balls.
3. Place these sausage balls on a baking sheet, baking for twenty minutes. Serve warm or chilled.

Pesto Bombs

Serves: 6

Time: 2 Hours 5 Minutes

Calories: 123

Protein: 4.3 Grams

Fat: 12.9 Grams

Net Carbs: 1.3 Grams

Ingredients:

- 1 Cup Cream Cheese, Full Fat
- 2 Tablespoons Basil Pesto
- 10 Green Olives, Sliced
- ½ Cup Parmesan Cheese, Grated

Directions:

1. Mix all ingredients together, serving it as a dip with cucumber slices.

Herbed Cheese Bites

Serves: 5
Time: 40 Minutes
Calories: 164
Protein: 3.7 Grams
Fat: 17.1 Grams
Net Carbs: 1.7 Grams
Ingredients:

- ¼ Cup Butter
- 3.5 Ounces Cream Cheese, Full Fat
- 4 Pieces Sun Dried Tomatoes, Drained & Chopped
- 4 Green Olives, Pitted & Chopped
- 2 Teaspoons Herbs, Dried
- 2 Cloves Garlic, Crushed
- 5 Tablespoon Parmesan Cheese, Grated
- Sea Salt & Black Pepper to Taste

Directions:

1. Blend your butter and cream cheese together, and then add in all of your ingredients except for your parmesan cheese. Mix well, and then refrigerate for a half hour.
2. Roll in parmesan cheese before serving.

Pork Belly Bombs

Serves: 6
Time: 40 Minutes
Calories: 263 **Protein:** 3.5 Grams
Fat: 26.4 Grams **Net Carbs:** 0.3 Grams
Ingredients:

- ¼ Cup Mayonnaise
- 5.3 Ounces Pork Belly, Cooked
- 3 Bacon Slices, Cut in Half
- 1 Tablespoon Horseradish, Fresh & Grated
- 1 Tablespoon Dijon Mustard
- 6 Lettuce Leaves for Serving
- Sea Salt & Black Pepper to Taste

Directions:

1. Preheat your oven to 325, and then cook your bacon for a half hour. Allow it to cool, and then crumble your bacon. Place it in a dish.
2. Shred your pork belly, placing it in a bowl.
3. Add in your mayonnaise, horseradish, and mustard. Mix well and season with salt and pepper.
4. Divide this mixture into six mounds, and then roll it in your crumbled bacon.
5. Serve on lettuce leaves.

Cheesy Artichoke Bombs

Serves: 4 **Time:** 50 Minutes
Calories: 408 **Protein:** 6.6 Grams
Fat: 39.6 Grams **Net Carbs:** 4 Grams
Ingredients:

- 2 Bacon Slices
- 2 Tablespoons Ghee
- 1 Clove Garlic, Minced
- ½ Onion, Large, Peeled & Diced
- 1/3 Cup Artichoke Hearts, Canned & Sliced
- ¼ Cup Sour Cream
- 1 Tablespoon Lemon Juice, Fresh
- ¼ Cup Mayonnaise
- ¼ Cup Swiss Cheese, Grated
- 4 Avocado Halves, Pitted
- Sea Salt & Black Pepper to Taste

Directions:

1. Fry your bacon for five minutes. It should be crisp. Allow it to cool before crumbling it and placing it in a bowl. Set the bowl to the side.
2. Cook your garlic and onion in the same pan using your ghee for three minutes.
3. Combine this in with your bacon, and then throw in your remaining ingredients.
4. Mix well, seasoning with salt and pepper. Refrigerate your mixture for a half hour before filling each avocado half with one.

Sausage & Avocado Bombs

Serves: 4 **Time:** 55 Minutes
Calories: 419 **Protein:** 11.4 Grams
Fat: 38.9 Grams **Net Carbs:** 2.7 Grams
Ingredients:

- 3.5 Ounces Spanish Chorizo Sausage, Diced
- ¼ Cup Butter, Unsalted
- 2 Hardboiled Eggs, Large & Diced
- 2 Tablespoons Mayonnaise
- 2 Tablespoons Chives, Chopped
- 1 Tablespoon Lemon Juice, Fresh
- 4 Avocado Halves, Pitted
- Sea Salt to Taste
- Cayenne Pepper to Taste

Directions:

1. Fry your chorizo over heat for five minutes before placing it to the side.
2. Get out a bowl and combine all of your ingredients, mashing it together. Make sure not to add in your avocado halves. They're for serving.
3. Refrigerate this mixture for a half hour before filling each avocado half. Serve chilled.

Ranch & Bacon Bombs

Serves: 4 **Time:** 2 Hours 30 Minutes
Calories: 419 **Protein:** 11.4 Grams
Fat: 38.9 Grams **Net Carbs:** 2.7 Grams
Ingredients:

- 1 Tablespoon Ranch Dressing Mix, Dry
- 8 Ounces Cream Cheese, Full Fat & Softened
- 2 Slices Bacon

Directions:

1. Start by heating your oven to 375, and then cook your bacon strips. They should take about fifteen minutes. Allow it to cool before crumbling it.

2. Get out a bowl and combine your cream cheese and ranch dressing mix. Stir in your bacon, and mix well.

3. Refrigerate for two hours before serving.

Vegetable Cheese Balls

Serves: 6 **Time:** 55 Minutes
Calories: 166 **Protein:** 3.4 Grams
Fat: 16.7 Grams **Net Carbs:** 3 Grams
Ingredients:
- ½ Onion, Peeled & Chopped
- ½ Cup Porcini Mushrooms, Dried
- 1 Tablespoon Ghee
- ¼ Cup Butter, Unsalted
- 3.5 Ounces Cream Cheese, Full Fat
- 1 Clove Garlic, Chopped Fine
- 2 Cups Spinach
- Sea Salt & Black Pepper to Taste
- ¼ Cup Hard Goat Cheese, Grated

Directions:
1. Throw your butter and cream cheese in a food processor until blended well.
2. Get a pan out and cook your garlic and onion using your ghee over medium heat. It should take three minutes, and then add in your spinach and mushrooms, cooking for another three minutes. Set it to the side so it cools.
3. Mix your butter and cream cheese with the spinach mixture, seasoning with salt and pepper. Refrigerate it for a half hour, and make it into five hours. Roll it into your goat cheese before serving.

Chive & Blue Cheese Bombs

Serves: 6 **Time:** 45 Minutes
Calories: 157 **Protein:** 5 Grams
Fat: 16.2 Grams **Net Carbs:** 0.8 Grams
Ingredients:

- ¼ Cup Butter, Unsalted
- ½ Cup Blue Cheese, Crumbled
- 3.5 Ounces Cream Cheese, Full Fat
- 2 Spring Onions, Chopped
- 1/3 Cup Chives, Fresh & Chopped
- 1 Tablespoon Parsley, Chopped

Directions:

1. Throw your butter and cream cheese in a food processor, mixing until well blended.

2. Add in all of your remaining ingredients except for chives, making sure it's mixed well.

3. Place this mixture in the fridge for a half hour, and roll in chives before serving.

Ham & Cheese Bombs

Serves: 6 **Time** 45 Minutes
Calories: 167 **Protein:** 6.4 Grams
Fat: 16.7 Grams **Net Carbs:** 0.7 Grams
Ingredients:

- ¼ Cup Butter, Unsalted
- ¼ Cup Cheddar Cheese, Grated
- 3.5 Ounces Cream Cheese, Full Fat
- 2 Tablespoons Basil, Fresh & Chopped
- 6 Slices Parma Ham
- 6 Green Olives, Large & Pitted
- Black Pepper to Taste

Directions:

1. Use a food processor to blend your butter and cream cheese together.
2. Add your basil and cheddar cheese, mixing well season with black pepper, and then place it in the fridge for a half hour.
3. Make six balls from your mixture, and then roll each one in Parma ham, topping with an olive to serve. You'll need a toothpick to hold the olive in place.

Olive & Tomato Bombs

Serves: 6 **Time:** 45 Minutes
Calories: 178 **Protein:** 4.2 Grams
Fat: 18.1 Grams **Net Carbs:** 1.9 Grams
Ingredients:

- ¼ Cup Sun dried Tomatoes, Drained & Chopped
- ¼ Cup Manchego Cheese, Grated
- 3.5 Ounces Cream Cheese, Full Fat
- ¼ Cup Butter, Unsalted
- ¼ Cup Green Olives, Pitted & Sliced
- 2 Tablespoons Capers, Drained
- 1/3 Cup Flaked Almonds
- 1 Clove Garlic, Crushed
- Black Pepper to Taste

Directions:

1. Use a food processor to blend your butter and cream cheese together until smooth.
2. Add in all of your remaining ingredients except for your almond flakes, and then mix well. Refrigerate for at least a half hour before serving, and then make six balls out of the mixture.
3. Roll each one into your almond flakes before serving.

Bacon & Cheese Bombs

Serves: 35 **Time:** 10 Minutes

Calories: 275 **Protein:** 0 Grams

Fat: 31 Grams **Net Carbs:** 1 Gram

Ingredients:

- 35 Slices Bacon
- 16 Ounces Mozzarella Cheese, Shredded
- 8 Tablespoons Almond Flour
- 8 Tablespoons Butter, Grass Fed
- 6 Tablespoons Psyllium Husk Powder (Or Flaxseed)
- ¼ Teaspoon Onion Powder
- ¼ Teaspoon Garlic Powder
- 1 Egg
- 2 Cups Butter, Grass Fed
- Sea Salt & Black Pepper to Taste

Directions:

1. Melt your butter and half of your mozzarella cheese in a double boiler. Add in your egg, beating it with a fork until smooth.

2. Add your remaining ingredients except for your bacon and remaining cheese. Make sure to mix well, and then take the mixture off of heat.

3. It should have a dough like constancy. Allow it to cool and then roll it out in a flat triangle.

4. Spread the remaining cheese on half of your dough before folding it over. The cheese should be in the middle.

5. Fold it over again, sealing it with your hands.

6. Cut into thirty-five squares.

7. Wrap each piece with bacon, and then heat up your oil in a pot to deep fry it.

8. Brown until crispy.

Crab Rangoon Bombs

Serves: 12 **Time:** 40 Minutes
Calories: 227 **Protein:** 13.8 Grams
Fat: 2.1 Grams **Net Carbs:** 0.6
Ingredients:
- 8 Ounces Cream Cheese
- 1 Can Crab
- ½ Teaspoon Garlic Powder
- ½ Teaspoon Onion Powder
- ½ Teaspoon Garlic, Minced
- ¾ Cup Mozzarella Cheese, Shredded
- 10 Slices Bacon
- Sea Salt & Black Pepper to Taste

Directions:
1. Heat your oven to 325, and then get out a baking sheet. Line it with parchment paper, and then bake for thirty minutes.
2. Allow your bacon to cool before you crumble it. Set it to the side, and then mix all of your remaining ingredients in a bowl.
3. Allow it to cool for a half hour, and then make twenty-four balls.
4. Roll them in your crumbled bacon before serving.

Buffalo Chicken Bites

Serves: 6 **Time:** 10 Minutes
Calories: 201 **Protein:** 18.8 Grams
Fat: 12.2 Grams **Net Carbs:** 0 Grams
Ingredients:

- 6 Ounces Chicken, Canned & Drained
- 8 Ounces Cream Cheese, Softened
- 2 Tablespoons Hot Sauce
- 1 Teaspoon Black Pepper
- 1 Teaspoon Paprika
- ¼ Teaspoon Cayenne Pepper
- 2 ½ Ounces Buffalo Flavored Walnuts
- 3 Slices Bacon, Thick Cut

Directions:
1. Sauté your bacon in a skillet and then drain on a paper towel.
2. Once it's cooled, crumble your bacon and place it in a bowl.
3. Get out another bowl and mix all of your remaining ingredients together. Add in your bacon. Chill for at least a half hour.
4. Chop your walnuts, putting them in a different bowl.
5. Make small balls out of your chicken mixture, and then roll your ball sin your walnuts.

Parmesan & Olive Bombs

Serves: 6
Time: 10 Minutes

Calories: 244

Protein: 1.2 Grams

Fat: 17.4 Grams

Net Carbs: 2.1 Grams

Ingredients:

- 5 Ounces Cream Cheese
- 1 Teaspoon Garlic, Minced
- 2 Tablespoons Parmesan Cheese
- ¼ Teaspoon Sea Salt, Fine
- 6 Olives, Chopped

Directions:

1. Mix your cream cheese, salt, garlic, and chopped olives together.
2. Make six balls, and roll in your parmesan cheese.
3. Refrigerate before serving.

Baked Brie Bombs

Serves: 4 **Time:** 25 Minutes
Calories: 127 **Protein:** 21.5 Grams
Fat: 23.5 Grams **Net Carbs:** 3.2 Grams
Ingredients:

- 6 Pecan Halves
- 1 Ounce Brie Cheese, Full Fat
- 1 Slice Prosciutto
- 1/8 Teaspoon Black Pepper

Directions:

1. Heat your oven to 350, and then fold your sliced prosciutto to make a square. Put it in a muffin tin, adding your brie cubes on top.

2. Sprinkle your pecan halves and pepper on next.

3. Bake for twelve minutes, and allow it to cool before serving.

Sesame Bombs

Serves: 6 **Time:** 12 Minutes
Calories: 248 **Protein:** 2.9 Grams
Fat: 15.7 Grams **Net Carbs:** 0.4 Grams
Ingredients:
- 4 Ounces Butter, Room Temperature
- 1 Teaspoon Sea Salt, Fine
- ¼ Teaspoon Chili Flakes
- 2 Teaspoons Sesame Seeds, Toasted
- 2 Tablespoons Sesame Oil

Directions:
1. Roast your sesame seeds in a skillet until golden brown. It should take two minutes. Set your sesame seeds to the side.
2. Mix your butter, sesame oil and chili flakes in a bowl, and then place the mixture into the fridge for fifteen minutes.
3. Make small balls, and roll them in your sesame seeds. Serve chilled.

Cheesy Cupcake

Serves: 1 **Time:** 6 Minutes
Calories: 492 **Protein:** 18 Grams
Fat: 49 Grams **Net Carbs:** 3 Grams
Ingredients:

- ½ Teaspoon Baking Powder
- ¼ Teaspoon Cayenne Pepper
- 1 Tablespoon Green Chilies, Chopped
- 3 Tablespoons Almond Meal
- 2 Tablespoons Butter, Grass Fed
- 2 Tablespoons Cheddar Cheese, Shredded
- 1 Egg
- Pinch Sea Salt

Directions:

1. Whisk your egg, and then add it to a microwave safe mug
2. Mix your softened butter and cheese together with your egg.
3. Add in all of your remaining ingredients, mixing well.
4. Microwave for a minute, and then eat warm.

Fried Cheese

Serves: 12 **Time:** 10 Minutes
Calories: 243 **Protein:** 16 Grams
Fat: 19 Grams **Net Carbs:** 0 Grams
Ingredients:

- 2 lbs. Queso Fresco
- 2 Tablespoons Coconut Oil
- 1 Tablespoon Basil, Fresh & Chopped
- 1 Tablespoon Olive Oil

Directions:

1. Heat your olive oil in a pan before cutting your cheese into small cubes.

2. Fry your cheese cubes in oil, making sure that all sides are browned.

3. Sprinkle with basil before serving.

Spicy Jalapeno Bombs

Serves: 12 **Time:** 35 Minutes
Calories: 207 **Protein:** 5 Grams
Fat: 19 Grams **Net Carbs:** 1 Gram
Ingredients:

- 12 Ounces Cream Cheese, Full Fat
- ¾ Teaspoon Garlic Powder
- ¾ Teaspoon Onion Powder
- 1 ½ Teaspoons Parsley, Dried
- 12 Bacon Slices
- 3 Jalapeno Peppers
- ¼ Teaspoon Sea Salt, Fine
- Black Pepper to Taste

Directions:

1. Fry your bacon. It should be crispy, and then chop until small.

2. Slice your jalapenos thin, and then soften your cream cheese.

3. Combine all of your ingredients together, and then chill them for a half hour before serving.

Pizza Bites

Serves: 12 **Time:** 20 Minutes
Calories: 110 **Protein:** 2 Grams
Fat: 11 Grams **Net Carbs:** 2 Grams
Ingredients:

- 14 Pepperoni Slices, Beef
- 2 Tablespoons Basil, Fresh & Chopped
- 2 Tablespoons Pesto
- 8 Olives, Pitted
- 8 Button Mushrooms
- 4 Ounces Mascarpone Cheese
- Sea Salt & Black Pepper to Taste

Directions:

1. Slice your mushrooms, olives and pepperoni into small pieces, and then get out a pan.
2. Cook your mushrooms for two to three minutes. They should brown, and then place them to the side to cool.
3. Get out a bowl and combine your pesto, salt, pepper and cheese.
4. Add in all remaining ingredients, and mix well.
5. Form into balls before serving. Store in the fridge until you're ready to eat the remainder.

Garlic & Cheese Bombs

Serves: 12 **Time:** 1 Hour 10 Minutes

Calories: 141 **Protein:** 9 Grams

Fat: 11 Grams **Net Carbs:** 1 Gram

Ingredients:

- 4 Tablespoons Butter, Grass Fed
- 1 Cup Keto Bread Crumbs
- 4 Cups Mozzarella, Shredded
- 2 Teaspoons Garlic Paste
- 2 Teaspoons Cilantro Paste
- Sea Salt to Taste

Directions:

1. Combine all of your ingredients until it forms a dough like consistency.
2. Make twelve portions, and then roll them in your keto bread crumbs.
3. Allow them to set for one to two hours in the fridge before serving.

Cheesy Chive Bites

Serves: 12 **Time:** 5 Minutes

Calories: 38 **Protein:** 7 Grams

Fat: 3 Grams **Net Carbs:** Less than 1 Gram

Ingredients:

- ¼ Cup Chives, Fresh
- 2 ½ Ounces Cream Cheese, Full Fat
- Almond Flour
- Sea Salt to Taste

Directions:

1. Chop your chives thin and then soften your cream cheese. Mix all ingredients together to for balls.
2. Chill for thirty minutes in the fridge before serving.

Cranberry Goat Cheese Bombs

Serves: 12 **Time:** 1 Hour 10 Minutes
Calories: 125 **Protein:** 7 Grams
Fat: 10 Grams **Net Carbs:** 2 Grams
Ingredients:

- 6 Ounces Goat Cheese
- ¼ Cup Pecans, Chopped
- 2/3 Cup Cranberries, Dried
- 2 Tablespoons Parsley, Chopped
- Sea Salt to Taste

Directions:

1. Start by copping your cranberries.
2. Soften your cream cheese, adding in all remaining ingredients. Mix well.
3. Form small balls out of the mixture, and allow them to chill for at least forty-five minutes before serving.

Savory Salmon

Serves: 12 **Time:** 5 Minutes
Calories: 117 **Protein:** 3 Grams
Fat: 13 Grams **Net Carbs:** 1 Gram
Ingredients:

- 50 Grams Smoked Salmon Trimmings
- 1 Cup Mascarpone Cheese
- 1 Tablespoon Apple Cider Vinegar
- 2/3 Cup Butter, Grass Fed & Softened
- 1 Tablespoon Parsley, Fresh & Chopped
- Sea Salt to Taste

Directions:

1. Soften your cheese before mixing in your salt, parsley and vinegar. Make sure it's well combined.
2. Add in your salmon and butter, forming small balls.
3. Place your salmon bites on parchment paper, and refrigerate before serving.

Salmon Benny Bombs

Serves: 4 **Time:** 10 minutes
Calories: 295 **Protein:** 18.2 Grams
Fat: 23.5 Grams **Net Carbs:** 0.66 Grams
Ingredients:

- 2 Eggs
- 4 Ounces Smoked Salmon, Sliced
- 2 Tablespoons Chives, Fresh & Chopped
- ½ Tablespoon Butter, Salted
- Sea Salt & Black Pepper to Taste
- 2 Tablespoons Mayonnaise

Directions:

1. Fill a small pot with water, and boil your eggs.
2. Heat two teaspoons of butter into a skillet, adding your salmon slices in.
3. Sauté your salmon until it turns crispy, and then put it to the side.
4. Peel your eggs, placing them in a bowl, and mash them with a fork.
5. Add in half of your salmon, mayonnaise, chives, butter, salt and pepper. Mix well, making balls with the mixture.
6. Mix your remaining chives and salmon in a plate, and roll the balls in this mixture, making sure it's coated well.

Mayonnaise & Bacon Bombs

Serves: 6 **Time:** 20 Minutes
Calories: 202 **Protein:** 10.2 Grams
Fat: 13.7 Grams **Net Carbs:** 0 Grams
Ingredients:
- 4 Slices Bacon, Large
- 2 Tablespoons Mayonnaise
- ¼ Cup Butter, Softened
- 2 Eggs, Large
- Sea Salt & Black Pepper to Taste

Directions:
1. Heat your oven to 375, and then line a baking sheet with parchment paper
2. Place your bacon in a single layer, and bake for fifteen minutes.
3. Boil your eggs, and then transfer them to an ice bath. Peel them, and mash your eggs with butter.
4. Stir in your mayonnaise, and season with salt and pepper. Mix well, and then pour in your baking grease.
5. Chill for a half hour, and then crumble your bacon onto a plate.
6. Make six balls out of the gg mixture, rolling it in the bacon before serving.

Avocado & Egg Bombs

Serves: 6 **Time:** 20 Minutes
Calories: 235 **Protein:** 19.7 Grams
Fat: 10.7 Grams **Net Carbs:** 0 Grams
Ingredients:

- 4 Slices Bacon
- 1 Tablespoon Lime Juice, Fresh
- 1 Avocado, Small
- 4 Tablespoons Butter
- 1 Clove Garlic, Crushed
- 1 Tablespoon Onion, Diced
- 1 Tablespoon Cilantro, Fresh & Chopped
- 1 Chili Pepper, Small & Chopped Fine
- Sea Salt & Black Pepper to Taste

Directions:

1. Start by heating your oven to 375, and then line a baking sheet with parchment paper.
2. Cook your bacon for fifteen minutes, and make sure to boil your eggs.
3. Peel your eggs, and mash and combine with butter.
4. Stir in your avocado flesh, mixing and mashing well.
5. Add all of your remaining ingredients except for your bacon, and mix well. Refrigerate for a half hour.
6. Crumble your bacon on a plate, and roll your egg mixture into six balls.
7. Roll your balls into your crumbled bacon.

Cheesy Egg & Bacon Bombs

Serves: 4 **Time:** 15 Minutes
Calories: 216 **Protein:** 14.3 Grams
Fat: 24.5 Grams **Net Carbs:** 0.8 Grams
Ingredients:

- 4 Eggs, Whisked
- 2 Tablespoons Butter, Divided
- 3 Bacon Slices, Chopped
- Sea Salt & Black Pepper to Taste
- 1 ¼ Cups Cheddar Cheese, Shredded
- 5 Tablespoons Cream Cheese, Softened

Directions:

1. Sauté your bacon for eight minutes or until done, and then allow it to drain on paper towel.
2. Heat your oven to 400, and ten oil a nine inch pie plate.
3. Melt your butter in a skillet before adding in your eggs. Stir for five minutes, and season with salt and pepper.
4. Scramble your eggs, and then add in your shredded cheese.
5. Crumble your bacon into the plate, and then make balls out of your egg mixture.
6. Roll these balls into your crumbled bacon before serving.

Conclusion

Now you know everything you need to in order to create your own fat bombs, but you can start with one of these sweet or savory recipes! You now have fat bomb recipes for any time of the day so that you can stick to your ketogenic diet without giving into temptation. There's no more worry that you won't meet your fat requirements on the ketogenic diet to stay in ketosis and reap the benefits of the keto diet. Fat bombs making sticking to the keto diet ten times easier, so you're always set up for success.